The Aquinas Lecture, 1985

HUMAN ENDS AND HUMAN ACTIONS

An Exploration in St. Thomas's Treatment

Under the auspices of the
Wisconsin-Alpha Chapter of Phi Sigma Tau

by
ALAN DONAGAN

MARQUETTE UNIVERSITY PRESS
MILWAUKEE
1985

Library of Congress Catalogue Card Number: 84-063124

© Copyright 1985
Marquette University

ISBN 0-87462-153-4

T. S.   6-10-87

For
WILLIAM A. MAHONEY
and
VERNON RICE

Non potest igitur Deus sic esse finis rerum
quasi aliquid constitutum, sed solum quasi
aliquid praeexistens obtinendum

Prefatory

The Wisconsin-Alpha Chapter of Phi Sigma Tau, the National Honor Society for Philosophy at Marquette University, each year invites a scholar to deliver a lecture in honor of St. Thomas Aquinas.

The 1985 Aquinas Lecture, *Human Ends and Human Actions: An Exploration in St. Thomas's Treatment,* was delivered in the Todd Wehr Chemistry Building on Sunday, February 24, 1985, by Alan Donagan, Professor of Philosophy at the California Institute of Technology.

Professor Donagan was born in Melbourne, Australia in 1925. He was educated at Wesley College, Melbourne, at Queen's College, University of Melbourne, and the University of Oxford (Exeter College), where he received the B. Phil. degree in 1953. He holds an honorary doctorate from Ripon College (1983).

He has taught at the University of Western Australia (1946-48), at University College, Canberra, Australia (1949-55), at the University of Minnesota (1956-61), at Indiana University (1961-65), at the University of Illinois, Urbana (1966-69), at the University of Chicago (1970-84), and is presently at the California Institute of Technology. He served as chairman of the departments of philosophy at Minnesota and Indiana; he was the Phyllis Fay Horton Professor of Humanities at the University of Chicago from 1977-84.

Professor Donagan is a member of the American Philosophical Association, of the Institut International de Philosophie, of the Council of Philosophical Studies, of the Mind Association and of the Aristotelian Society. He was President of the American Philosophical Association, Western Division, 1980-81, and Chairman of the Council for Philosophical Studies, 1979-83.

His publications include over fifty articles that have appeared in prestigious journals, collections, and histories. His books are: *The Theory of Morality* (1977), *The Philosophy of History,* with Barbara Donagan (1965), *The Later Philosophy of R.G. Collingwood,* (1962). He has also edited and written an introduction to *Essays in the Philosophy of Art,* by R.G. Collingwood. In 1980 he delivered the Lindley Lecture at the University of Kansas, *Morality, Property and Slavery* (Lawrence, Kansas, 1981).

To Professor Donagan's distinguished list of publications, Phi Sigma Tau is pleased to add: *Human Ends and Human Actions: An Exploration in St. Thomas's Treatment.*

HUMAN ENDS AND HUMAN ACTIONS
An Exploration in St. Thomas's Treatment

1. The Two Teleologies

There are at least two different ways in which human beings explain one another's actions. One, the most common, is by treating the action to be explained as behavior with a purpose, and a purpose as an end to be brought about. When we know what somebody proposed to bring about when he acted in a certain fashion, and why he believed that so acting was, in his situation, the way to bring that end about, we can claim so far to understand his action. Philosophy furnishes us with a word for such explanations: the word 'teleological.' Human action is characteristically directed to *telē*, or ends; and a *telos* is an event of a certain kind to be made to happen, or (less accurately, I believe) a state of affairs of a certain kind to be brought about. Sometimes this event is fairly simple, such as at last getting in your first serve in a tennis game, after an ignominious string of failures; sometimes it is highly complex, such as living a happy life.

A second way of explaining human actions, although less common, is nevertheless familiar. You have match point in a tennis game against an opponent to whom you mostly lose, and he makes a nearly impossible return which only you are in a position to see. With much inward grief, you have to call "In!" You are not a moral masochist. Giving calls against yourself in such situations is not one of your purposes in life. And yet we understand your doing it, even if, in your shoes, we should not have. How do we understand it? Perhaps, to begin with, in terms of fairness and sportsmanship. But what lies behind the rules of fairness and sportsmanship? Is it not simply that your opponent is somebody to whom you owe the truth, miserable wretch though he is for bringing that return off? You acted for his sake, not to realize any purpose of your own.

The phrase "for his sake" is inescapably teleological. It signifies that on account of which your action was done. You did what you did, not for any outcome it might have pro-

duced, but out of concern for your opponent.
You were certainly not concerned to concede
him the point. If his return had been in and
neither he nor you had seen it, you would not
have repined at all. Yet, for his sake, you
regarded cheating as out. Your opponent was
the end of your action in a way quite different
from that in which any purpose you had might
have been.

Even so, is not the fundamental sense of
'telos' the first: that of an event to be made
to happen? Not for St. Thomas, as we shall
see. But that is not immediately evident in
his language, as it was to be in the language
of his great successor, the blessed John Duns
Scotus. Scotus distinguished *finis,* an end
(that is *telos*) from what he called *'finitum,'*
literally an 'ended,' namely, that which stands
to an end as that which is brought about
stands to what brings it about.

> [A] *finitum* depends for its being upon a *finis* as
> [essentially] prior [Scotus declared] just to the extent
> that the *finis* as loved moves an efficient [cause] to
> confer being on it.

And so, he proceeds,

> a corollary follows, which should not be passed over in silence, namely, that a certain opinion about the *finis* is a *falsa imaginatio*. [That opinion is] that the final cause of a being is the last operation [in causing it], or the object brought about through that operation. [1]

His line of thought, I take it, is this. Sometimes, as in official or productive activity, the end of an action is either the last operation performed (such as the granting of an official permission), or is something produced by that operation (such as a finished product turned off an assembly line); but in neither case do the actions that lead up to the end depend on it as essentially prior to them, for it is prior to them only as something thought by the agent or designer. By contrast, when the end of an action is essentially prior to it, it cannot be either an operation that forms part of it or something produced by it. It can only be a pre-existent thing that is loved by the agent, and for the sake of which he acts. And an ultimate end must be essentially prior to any action of which it is the end.

It is evident that the two kinds of *telos* disclosed by these examples are connected with two different conceptions of morality. Events to be brought about are *telē* of the kind that are recognized in consequentialist conceptions of it, and persons are *telē* of the kind that are recognized in conceptions of it as a limit to be observed in trying to realize our purposes.

Anybody who, like myself, is interested in these two kinds of *telos* will be refreshed by St. Thomas's treatment of the ends of human action in both his moral philosophy and his moral theology. For, unlike most of our contemporaries, he did not embrace one of the two kinds of *telos* and ignore the other. Nobody has reaffirmed more emphatically than he the Aristotelian doctrine that "all men agree in seeking an ultimate end, which is happiness *(beatitudo)*."[2] Nor has anybody confessed more passionately than he the Mosaic and Christian faith that "the end of human life and society is God."[3] And God is not, as some process theologians would have us believe, an event to be brought about.

Unfortunately, I have not enough learning to investigate St. Thomas's teleology of human action thoroughly and systematically. At best, I can lead you on a free ramble through some things he wrote about it in the two of his works with which I am least unfamiliar: the two *Summae*. Even here, when the mountain air makes breathing hard for me, I shall retreat to the valleys of more recent philosophy. However, as you will see, that is not because I think any philosopher to have done better that St. Thomas on the questions I shall consider. My hope is that I may irritate somebody better equipped into providing us with something more systematic.

2. The Two Teleologies in St. Thomas

St. Thomas's commitment to both of the kinds of teleology I have distinguished is evident in what he had to say about the difference between the relation of intellectual creatures to what he referred to as "the ultimate end of the whole of things" and that of non-intellectual ones. "Only the intellectual creature reaches the very ultimate end of the whole of things through his own operation, which is the knowing and loving of God: whereas other creatures cannot attain the ultimate end except by a participation in its likeness" (*Summa contra Gentiles* III, 111, 1). Here, while the ultimate end of the whole of things is unmistakably God, presumably the operation by which intellectual creatures reach that end is also an end for them. God is indeed the being for whose sake they act, but the operation by which he is attained is an event they aim at bringing about.

Although the cheerful remark I have quoted from the *Summa contra Gentiles* seems clear enough, it must be acknowledged that some philosophers have found it difficult to conceive how any existing being can be an end. For example, Sir David Ross, the great British Aristotle scholar of the first half of our century, wrote, in another connection, the "an end is an object of desire, and an object of desire is something that does not yet exist."[4] If Ross were right, attaining an end could not be anything except bringing it into existence. And so it would be nonsensical to describe God, who exists now and always, as an end to be attained by rational creatures in one way, and by non-rational creatures in another.

Before we dismiss Ross's objection as fatuous, which I think it is, we should acknowledge that St. Thomas himself, when he wrote about the end of human life, as distinct from the end of the whole of things, usually referred to it as something not yet existing which we hope may be brought into existence. For example, in *Summa contra Gentiles* III,

25, 7, he wrote that

> a thing has the greatest desire for its ultimate end.
> Now, the human intellect has a greater desire, and
> love, and pleasure, in knowing divine matters than
> it has in the perfect knowledge of the lowest things,
> even though it can grasp but little concerning divine
> things. So, the ultimate end of man is to understand
> God, in some fashion.

Here the ultimate end of human beings in this life is presented as an object of desire that does not yet exist. And a little later in the same chapter St. Thomas went on to identify it with *felicitas,* the commonest equivalent in the *Summa contra Gentiles* of Aristotle's *eudaimonia.* Apparently, whatever his opinion may have been about the ultimate end of the whole of things, he agreed with Ross that the ultimate end of human beings in this life is to attain a state they have not yet attained.

How are such pairs of passages as these to be reconciled? One way would be this. The ultimate end of everything in each order of being – inanimate things, plants, brute animals, rational animals and separate substances – is to attain a state it is not in; and since those states are definable only by reference to God, God is the ultimate end of the whole of things in the sense that he and he alone is that by reference to which the ultimate ends of all things are defined. What is wrong with this will be evident to you. It is that there must be some reason why the ultimate ends of all things can be defined only by reference to God; and that reason must yield a deeper sense in which God is the ultimate end of the whole of things than that their specific ends can all be so defined. What is that deeper sense?

St. Thomas's first answer to this question in *Summa contra Gentiles* was metaphysical. An end is a final cause. From this it follows that

> the end holds first place over other types of cause, and to it all other causes owe the fact that they are causes in act: for the agent only acts for the sake of the end . . . . Therefore the ultimate end is the first cause of all (III, 17, 9).

And the first cause of all is, of course, God: the first cause, and the first agent. Now, St. Thomas continues,

> an end that is produced by the action of an agent cannot be the first agent; it is, rather an effect of an agent. Therefore, God cannot be the end of things in this way, as something produced (*constitutum*), but only as something pre-existing (*praeexistens*) to be obtained (III, 18, 3).

The ultimate end of human action, or of action
of any other kind, cannot be something that
does not yet exist, if that end is, as all good
Aristotelians believe, the ultimate final cause.
Hence we must distinguish between the end
of an action, which exists before it, and what
St. Thomas calls the 'obtaining' of that end.
Obtaining the end is not the end. Nor does
'obtaining,' as St. Thomas uses it here, stand
for any kind of exclusive ownership or
dominion.

Of course, this line of thought does not find
favour with many metaphysicians today. And
on this point I imagine that most of us here,
including many who would call themselves
Thomists, stand with the majority of our contemporaries. If we accept, as I do, St.
Thomas's doctrine that God is something like
the final cause of things as that is conceived
in Aristotle's metaphysics (of course that is
not all he is), it is not for Aristotle's reason,
that the universe has a final *natural* cause.
For what reason then? I believed that St.
Thomas gets at it in an observation about the
ends of productive actions generally.

> [T]he ultimate end of any maker, as a maker, is
> himself; it is for our own sakes that we use things
> made by us, and if sometimes a man makes a thing

for some other purpose, this has reference to his own good, either as useful, or delectable, or right (*honestum*).

Now, what holds for all makers holds for God.

God is the productive cause of all things . . . . Therefore, he himself is the end of all things (III, 17, 8).

This argument implies that creatures as well as God may be ends. Later in the third Part of *Summa contra Gentiles* St. Thomas went on to draw that conclusion when he came to address himself to the foundations of morality. Rational creatures excel all others not only in the dignity of their end, but also in the perfection of their nature.

In perfection of nature, only the rational creature has dominion over its acts, freely moving itself to doing them *(ad operandum)*. Other creatures are moved to the activities *(opera)* proper to them rather than move [themselves to them] (III, 111, 1).

Among creatures, only the intellectual ones (St. Thomas uses the words 'rational' and 'intellectual' interchangeably in this connection) are principal agents, as distinct from instruments.

What is moved only by another has the nature *(ratio)* of an instrument: but what is moved *per se* has the nature of a principal agent. Now, an instrument is

wanted, not for its own sake *(propter seipsum),* but
so that a principal agent may use it. Hence all the
careful work that is devoted to instruments must
be referred to the principal agent as end; but what
is done for the principal agent, either by himself or
by another, is for his sake *(propter ipsum),* inasmuch
as he is a principal agent. Therefore intellectual
creatures are treated by God as things cared about
(procuratae) for their own sakes . . . (III, 112, 1).

To this, St. Thomas added a parallel argument: namely, that intellectual creatures are
ends – things cared about for their own
sakes – not only as principal agents, but also
as attaining what they do through their own
efforts.

[W]henever things are ordered to any end, if any
among them cannot attain the end through their
own efforts *(per seipsa),* they must be subordinated
to those that attain it and are ordered to it for their
own sakes . . . . Now . . . God is the ultimate end of
the whole of things. An intellectual nature alone
attains to God in himself, that is, by knowing him
and loving him . . . . Therefore the intellectual
nature is the only one in the universe that is wanted
(quaesita) for its own sake, and all others for its sake
(III, 112, 3).

Moreover, creatures of intellectual nature are
wanted for their own sakes as individuals. "A
rational creature," St. Thomas declared,
"stands to divine providence as governed and

provided for for his own sake, not only for the sake of his species, as other corruptible creatures are" (III, 113, 2).

That rational beings as such are ends, creator and creature alike, is the foundation of the moral law. "Law is nothing but a certain reason and rule of operation (*ratio et regula operandi*)" (III, 114, 3). In governing themselves according to that reason and rule, human beings "participate in a certain likeness of divine providence" (III, 114, 2). But "the end of every law, and above all of divine law, is to make men good," and what makes a human being good is "possessing a good will" (III, 116, 3). A person of good will wills, first of all, "to cling to God . . . through love," and next, to love his neighbors (III, 116, 1 and 117, 1). That he do so, St. Thomas pointed out, is the sense of what St. Matthew's gospel recognizes as the two fundamental commandments on which the whole Mosaic Torah hangs (III, 116, 6 and 117, 7).

In explaining the reason of these commandments – that is, why they are laws – St. Thomas makes it clear that the first holds because God is an end: "the will is good because it wills a good object, and especially the greatest good, which is the end" (III, 116,

3). However, he does not make it as clear that the same is true of the second. Indeed, the reason he gave for it is easily mistaken for an anticipation of Hume's.

> [T]here ought (*oportet*) to be a union in affection among those for whom there is a common end [he wrote]. Now men share in common the one ultimate end which is happiness . . . . So, men ought to be united with each other by a mutual love (III, 117, 1).

And he continued,

> [I]t is natural to all men to love each other. A sign of this is that by a certain natural instinct, a man comes to the help of any man in need, even one he does not know . . . . Therefore, mutual love is prescribed for men by the divine law (III, 117, 6).

Unlike Hume, however, St. Thomas saw in natural instinct not a substitute for a requirement of practical reason, but a sign that such a requirement underlies it.[5] And his assertion that happiness (*beatitudo*) is the ultimate end shared by all men must be understood in the light of his doctrine that happiness itself presupposes a pre-existent end.

The structure of morality as St. Thomas presents it in *Summa contra Gentiles* accordingly seems to be this. God, the first cause and first agent, is the ultimate pre-existing end of the whole of things, before all produced ends (*fines constituti*). Rational creatures also, by the providence of God, act for their own sakes. But what their own sakes require is that they obtain the ultimate end of the whole of things by loving and understanding it. A necessary condition of their doing that is that their wills be good: that is, that they will according to law. Law is reason and rule. And reason and rule require, first of all, that they love God, and secondly, that they love their neighbors – all other rational beings. The Mosaic Torah lays down in detail what these fundamental commandments imply.

However, *Summa contra Gentiles,* written between 1258 and 1264, is one of St. Thomas's earlier works. In the later *Summa Theologiae,* written between 1266 and 1273, morality is treated much more elaborately, and at first sight, differently. The morality of *Summa contra Gentiles* is unmistakably a deontology based on a distinctive teleology of pre-existent ends; that in *Summa Theologiae* is for the most part a theory of virtues and vices based on a theory of right reason. Yet, despite the obvious differences of subject, differences of doctrine turn out to be largely in emphasis. [6]

A brief survey must suffice. That the treatise *de Lege* in *Summa Theologiae* (I-II, 90-97) expands the treatment of moral law in the earlier *Summa*, but without contradicting it, is as far as I know, not seriously questioned. What is called in *Summa contra Gentiles* "divine law," that is, the reason and rule of operation in which human beings participate in a certain likeness of divine providence, is now called "natural law (*lex naturalis*)" (*ST* I-II, 91, 2). And, as in *Summa contra Gentiles*, all the moral precepts of the Mosaic Torah are declared to be contained in the natural law, and to be summed up in the two *prima et communia praecepta,* 'Love God' and 'Love your neighbor' (*ST* I-II, 99, 1 ad 2; 100, 3). The additions to Mosaic moral teaching made by Christianity are declared to be few, and chiefly to be a matter of forbidding internal acts not forbidden in all cases by Moses (*ST* I-II, 107, 4).

That both God and human beings are recognized to be pre-existent ends in *Summa Theologiae* is equally evident. As far as morality is concerned, it is explicitly laid down that all morality arises from love of the pre-existent ends, God and human beings. St. Thomas commented on St. Paul's at first sight surprising assertion that "If there is any other commandment it is comprised in this saying: 'Thou shalt love thy neighbor as thyself,' " that

> [T]he whole of the law is summed up in this single commandment . . . as the end to which, in a certain sense, all the commandments are directed. For when one loves one's neighbor for God's sake, then this love includes the love of God also (*ST* I-II, 99, 1 ad 2).

I shall therefore assume that, early and late, St. Thomas thought of morality as a matter of law (law itself being understood as a matter of reason), and of law as resting on a teleology of pre-existent ends.

3. Human Tragedy and Philosophical Comedy

It is now time to return to a topic briefly introduced and then laid aside: St. Thomas's unwavering Aristotelian teaching that "the ultimate end of man, and of every intellectual substance, is called *felicitas* or *beatitudo;* for this is what every intellectual substance desires as [its] ultimate end, and for its own sake alone" (*Summa contra Gentiles,* III, 25, 14). Can St. Thomas reconcile this with the Christian doctrine that the ultimate end of human action is not something brought about by it, but something that pre-exists it?

The chief difficulty in doing so is that, according to Aristotle, happiness or blessedness – *eudaimonia* or *to makarion* in Greek, *felicitas* or *beatitudo* in Latin – is something rational beings naturally seek. As we shall see, there turn out to be difficulties in this concept that compel a distinction within it. Still, what do human beings naturally seek? Aristotle's answer to this question is well known, but worth repeating:

> human good turns out to be activity of soul in accordance with virtue, and if there are more than one virtue, in accordance with the best and most complete. But we must add 'in a complete life.' For one swallow does not make a summer, nor does one day; and so too one day, or a short time, does not make a man blessed and happy (*Eth. Nic.* I, 1098a 16-19).

On any unsentimental view of the conditions of human life, two grim consequences follow. The first is that, since they will not receive the nurture and training of a free citizen of an Hellenic *polis* – and that is what is necessary for engaging in activity in accordance with virtue – many human beings will never have the capacity to attain the human good. The second is that, since not even capacity and virtue together ensure good fortune in

this world, the virtuous and able will sometimes fail to attain it.

Human life, as Aristotle conceived it, is inescapably tragic. Some individual lives are
happy; but nobody, however great or noble,
can count on it.

[A] multitude of great events . . . if they turn out
ill . . . crush and maim blessedness (*to makarion*);
for they both bring pain with them and hinder many
activities . . . . [T]he man who is truly good and wise,
we think, bears all the chances of life becomingly
and always makes the best of circumstances . . . .
And if this is the case, the happy man (*ho eudaimon*)
can never become miserable (*athlios*) – though he
will not reach blessedness (*makarios*), if he meet
with fortunes like those of Priam (*Eth. Nic.* I, 1100b
25-1101a 8).

No doubt it is better to have been Hector or
Priam than to have been a lifelong slave; but
to say that a tragic hero like Hector attained
the end of human life would be absurd.

Aristotle's investigation has led him to
distinguish two varieties of ultimate human
good: a happiness attainable by anybody
whose nurture and training has endowed him
with the capacity for virtuous action – a happiness he calls *eudaimonia;* and a happiness
for which luck in needed as well, which he
calls *to makarion*. Neither is palatable to a

Christian or post-Christian mind, for whom
no human being should be conceived as ex-
cluded from the human good. Yet is there any
alternative? Light is thrown on St. Thomas's
medieval rejection of Aristotle's tragic view
by the vain struggles of two representative
modern philosophers, Immanuel Kant and
Henry Sidgwick, to find such an alternative.

Both Kant and Sidgwick found the tragic
view of life unacceptable because of what they
believed to be demands of practical reason.
Both maintained that practical reason imposes on those who have it two distinct principles, which would generate inconsistent
precepts unless certain further postulates
were true. Since rational creatures cannot
practically reject those principles, neither can
they practically refuse to postulate what is
necessary for their reconciliation.

Since Sidgwick's reasoning is more elemen-
tary, I begin with it. Of the two principles
which he believed practical reason to impose,
the first is universalistic: namely, the utili-
tarian greatest happiness principle, that
among the courses of action open to him, a
truly rational agent would choose one that
would produce the greatest amount of happiness on the whole.[7] If he had thought that

practical reason imposed no principle but this, Sidgwick would not have questioned the finality of the verdict of experience that life is tragic. After all, most human beings, for no apparent fault of theirs, do not lead lives that are happy on the whole; and, owing to their inescapable ignorance of many effects of the different courses of action open to them, even those who sincerely try to act on the greatest happiness principle often do not succeed. But Sidgwick was convinced that practical reason also imposes a second principle: namely, the egoist one that a truly rational agent would always choose, among the courses open to him, one from which he would get for himself the greatest surplus of pleasure over pain. [8] It would profit nothing to examine either Sidgwick's reasons for this principle, or how he answered objections to it. Both, in my opinion, have worn at least as well as his reasons for the greatest happiness principle. What matters here is that Sidgwick believed that this "dualism of practical reason," as Schneewind has called it, gives us ground to reject the finality of tragedy in life. [9] Why did he believe that?

Sidgwick allowed that philosophy can tolerate the world's being so ordered that what practical reason demands that we try to attain is in fact unattainable. But he dismissed as ridiculous any suggestion that practical reason might demand the logically impossible in any situation to which its precepts apply. In themselves, his two principles of practical reason do not collide. It may be that, in any situation to which they apply, a course of action that will yield the greatest amount of happiness on the whole may be identical with one from which the agent would get for himself the greatest surplus of pleasure over pain. Unfortunately, experience leaves no doubt that this is not always so. Yet if any human being should ever be confronted with a situation in which he could not get for himself the greatest surplus of pleasure over pain by an action that would yield the greatest amount of happiness on the whole, then, on Sidgwick's principles, practical reason would demand of him both that he do something that would yield the greatest amount of happiness on the whole, and that he not do it. And in that case, there would be "a fundamental contradiction in one chief department of our thought" – namely, ethics. [10]

Sidgwick therefore held that our practical reason feels a "vital need" to "prov[e] or postulat[e]" a "connexion of Virtue and self-interest, if it is to be made consistent with itself."[11] But is this vital need a philosophical necessity? Proving it seems out of the question. Are we then entitled to postulate it? Only if we are entitled to postulate that there cannot be contradictions in fundamental departments of our thought; and Sidgwick acknowledged that whether we are or not is "profoundly difficult and controverted."[12] However, there are those who hold that "the edifice of physical science is really constructed of conclusions logically inferred from self-evident premises" – Sidgwick himself was so inclined – and if they are right, if "in our supposed knowledge of the world of nature propositions are commonly taken to be universally true, which yet seem to rest on no other grounds than that we have a strong disposition to accept them, and that they are indispensable to the systematic coherence of our beliefs," then, Sidgwick declared, "it will be more difficult to reject a similarly supported assumption in ethics, without opening the door to universal scepticism."[13]

Such a conclusion is less convincing than astonishing. If intuitively held principles generate a contradiction, then the beliefs to which they give rise cannot be systematically coherent, and one or more of them must be false. The natural inference from Sidgwick's argument is not that his principles must be supernaturally reconciled, but that something must be wrong with one or both of them. St. Thomas, it is hardly necessary to say, would have dismissed both.

Kant's variation on the same theme is more persuasive, because he made no mention of intuitively self-evident principles. Instead, he began by distinguishing two senses in which a good can be the 'highest.' A good may be *supreme,* that is, there may be no other to which it is subordinate; or it may be *perfect (consummatum),* that is, it may be a whole that is no part of a larger whole. A good will, that is, a will that wills for the sake of duty, is the supreme good: it is subordinate to no other, and is the sole necessary condition of anything's being unqualifiedly good. But it is not the perfect or complete good. For that

> happiness is also required, and indeed not merely in the partial eyes of a person who makes himself his end, but even in the judgement of an impartial reason, which in general regards persons in the world as ends-in-themselves. For to be in need of happiness and also worthy of it and yet not partake of it could not be in accordance with the complete

> volition of an omnipotent rational being, if we
> assume such for the sake of the argument. [14]

Now, "even though they belong to a highest good which they jointly make possible," virtue (good will) and happiness are distinct, and the maxims *Pursue virtue* and *Pursue happiness* are "wholly heterogeneous and far from being at one in respect to their supreme practical principle."[15] Nevertheless,

> Since . . . the furthering of the highest good, which
> contains [the] connection [of virtue with happiness]
> in its concept, is an a priori necessary object of our
> will and is inseparably related to the moral law, the
> impossibility of the former must prove the falsity
> of the latter also. [16]

Yet practical reason cannot entertain the possibility that the moral law is false. It must therefore postulate whatever is necessary to avoid entertaining it. And two postulates are necessary: the immortality of the soul (so that a virtuous person's failure to attain happiness in this life will not be final), and the existence of God (so that the after-life will not repeat the failure of the present one).

This is not the place for an adequate appraisal of Kant's argument: for that I recommend Allen W. Wood's sympathetic study, *Kant's Moral Religion.*[17] However, I beg to draw your attention to a feature of it that bears on what St. Thomas would have thought of it. The theoretical possibility Kant rejects as practically absurd is that a virtuous man be required by practical reason to seek the highest good – the union of virtue and happiness – in a world in which he cannot attain it. But is any human being virtuous in the sense in question? Certainly there are those who have lived virtuous lives by ordinary human standards, and even those who have acted with heroic virtue in circumstances in which almost nobody would have; but were their wills unwaveringly good in all circumstances? If not, does the question of Kant's *absurdum practicum* arise at all?

In his later writings on religion, as Wood points out, Kant acknowledged that

> in spite of the differing conditions in which we find man, a propensity to evil, to lie, to kill his fellows, or to enslave and exploit them, to adopt any course of action which leads to the satisfaction of personal wishes, is always characteristic of him. And hence Kant conclude[d] that each of us has grounds for saying, in the words of Romans 3:9: "They are all under sin, – there is none righteous, no, not one."[18]

Well, if none are virtuous, nothing in practice would follow from the world's being so ordered that, if any were virtuous, they would not be assured that they could attain happiness, and hence nothing absurd in practice would.

It does not follow, of course, that it is not our duty to strive for a more equitable distribution of happiness in the world, or that the misery many of the best of humankind have endured should not sicken us. But there is no practical absurdity in asserting, on one hand, that it is an absolute duty to act with good will, and to try to ensure happiness to all who do; and on the other, that among human beings, flawed individuals in flawed societies, the best will often fare worst. The best have never drawn the conclusion that, unless it is legitimate to postulate a supernatural world to redress the iniquities of the natural one, the duty to act with good will would be a chimera. Rather, they have agreed with Edgar, in Shakespeare's *King Lear,* that

Men must endure
Their going hence, ev'n as their coming hither:
Ripeness is all.

4. St. Thomas on the Limits of Aristotelian Eudaimonia

The happiness rational beings seek on principle, according to both Kant and Sidgwick, is natural. And Kant's account of natural happiness is in the main Aristotelian. (Sidgwick's was more hedonistic than is now fashionable.) I do not think we know how St. Thomas would have answered the question, 'Given that human beings are rational inhabitants of a natural universe, seeking happiness as Aristotle understood it, and that there are no non-ethical grounds for asserting the existence of anything supernatural, would there be any reason to suppose that the virtuous cannot be finally unhappy?' Since he believed himself to have demonstrated non-ethically that a natural universe cannot exist without a supernatural creator, he denied that the question could arise except on a false view of things; and he was not interested in answering such questions.

Even so, I think that St. Thomas would have acknowledged that false philosophical positions can be internally coherent. Hence I also think that he would have admitted that

the question I have asked arises. So, although
he neither answered it nor affirmed anything
from which an answer can be directly deduced,
it is not senseless to ask what a Thomistic answer to it would be. In the language of today,
I conjecture that it would be something like
this. "In deciding whether, on the false suppositions given, it is practically reasonable to
accept that the virtuous can be finally unhappy, two things must be remembered about
the human situation as, without revelation,
it would be reasonable to believe it to be. The
first is that the virtuous are far from completely virtuous. The second is that most of
the evils that afflict human beings are caused
by other human beings, and that there is no
evil in the wills of others that has not a coun-
terpart in our own. Given these facts, no
human being can say, 'The undeserved evil
that is done to me is done by beings with
whom I have no kinship, and is utterly unlike
anything I myself have willed.' This neither
excuses it nor makes that person in any way
responsible for it. But it does show that a
world of beings like ourselves is one in which
it is to be expected that the virtuous will often
be finally and irremediably unhappy. Yet it
does not follow that it is unreasonable to

strive to be virtuous. On the suppositions given, the finality of tragedy in human life must be accepted."

Of course, St. Thomas did not begin either where Aristotle did in the ancient world, or Kant and Sidgwick in the modern. While accepting, as common wisdom, that no human being in the present dispensation is wholly virtuous, they would all have dismissed as mythical his assumption, which he admitted cannot be philosophically demonstrated, that the innocent beings originally created were much more than free and guiltless of wrong-doing—much more than what Pelagius took human beings now to be. Contrary to both pre-Christian and post-Christian opinion, St. Thomas held that human beings in a state of innocence had,

> as Augustine says . . . *a tranquil avoidance of sin, and while that lasted, there could be no sort of evil at all* . . . . [F]rom the very rightness of that original state . . . as long as the soul remained subject to God, the inferior things in man would be put under the superior, and the superior would not be hindered by the inferior (*ST*, I, 94, 4c).

In this state, human beings know God "with a higher sort of knowledge than we do now; so [their] knowledge was somehow half way between (*media . . . inter*) knowledge in our present state and knowledge in the home-country *(patria),* where God is seen through [his] essence" *(ST,* I, 94, 1c). And this knowledge was not natural, that is, not by experience or connaturality: "the first man had knowledge of everything through ideas *(species)* infused by God" *(ST,* I, 94, 3 ad 1).

Why remind you of medieval notions that those among you who want St. Thomas to be taken seriously today may well prefer to forget? Mainly because Christianity as traditionally understood is committed to treating the myth of the Garden of Eden, which St. Thomas accepted literally, as expressing an anthropological truth. If traditional Christianity remains an intellectual option, then it remains an intellectual option that the state of human beings as we know it neither was original nor will be final. To inquire into the ultimate end of human life as though that is not an option flatly dismisses Christianity. I am unwilling to dismiss it, and I assume that you are too. But in that case, we must hold, with St. Thomas, that just as it would be a mistake to infer, with respect to the happiness they can attain, that human beings originally were what they now are, so it would be a mistake to infer that they always will be what they now are. St. Thomas took it to be a revealed truth that in their original state human beings once knew God by a half-way infused knowledge they can no longer have. And he also held that, in their *patria,* the world to come, they will know God directly.

What this direct knowledge will be they cannot know now. But in the *Summa contra Gentiles,* assuming the correctness of Aristotle's theory that human thought about anything is by way of something in the human mind that serves as an intelligible species of it, St. Thomas ventured to draw the following conclusions about it.

> [T]he divine essence may be related to the created intellect as an intelligible species by which it understands . . . . Yet, [the divine essence] cannot be the form of [a created intellect] in its natural being, for the result of this would be that, once joined to [that created intellect], it would make up one nature. This could not be, since the divine intellect is in itself perfect in its own nature. But an intelligible species, united with an intellect, does not make up a nature; rather, it perfects it for [an act of] understanding . . . . This immediate vision of God is promised us in Scripture: "We see now through a glass darkly; but then face to face" (I Cor. 13: 12). It is wrong to understand this in a corporeal way, picturing in our imagination a bodily face of the Divinity . . . . [W]e

shall see God face to face, in the sense that we shall
see him without a medium, as is true when we see
a man face to face (*SCG* III, 51, 4-5).

If we presuppose that a direct vision of God
is attainable by divine grace, and that it will
totally satisfy those who are granted it, then
our inquiry into what is the happiness that all
men seek is transformed.

There are two cases to consider. The first,
and philosophically the less interesting, is that
of those who believe the Christian revelation.
Even Aristotle, in a passage to which St.
Thomas drew attention, noted that because
eudaimonia is a *telos* that is 'telic' in every
way, even those who are active in accordance
with complete virtue, and are sufficiently
equipped with external goods throughout a
complete life, can only be said to be *makarioi*
as men are; for, since the future is always
obscure to them, their *eudaimonia* is not 'telic'
in every way.[19] By contrast, nobody who
believes the Christian revelation can seriously
imagine that those who see God face to face
can have anything more to want: their end
as intellectual beings would be completely attained (*ST* I-II, 3, 8c).

The more interesting case is that of those
who do not believe the Christian revelation.

St. Thomas's view of their state reminded me
of the analysis of desire generally offered by
Bertrand Russell in his *Analysis of Mind,* one
of the several volumes in which, according to
C.D. Broad, he "laboured . . . to make a coherent philosophy out of the thin crudities of
behaviourism."[20] According to Russell, what
is essential to desire is an initial state of a person (called 'discomfort') that gives rise to restless activity which continues until a new state
is reached in which restless activity ceases.
What is desired is not what the person believes he seeks, but what in fact puts an end
to his discomfort.[21] Now, according to St.
Thomas, although the only thing that will put
an end to the restless striving of human beings is the vision of God, most of them do not
know it. Moreover, except by revelation,
nobody can know it, not even those in a state
of innocence.

> [F]or the direction of one's own and others' lives,
> besides knowledge of things that can be learned
> naturally, one needs to know things beyond natural
> knowledge, because human life is directed to a cer-
> tain supernatural end; and so for the direction of our
> life it is necessary to know matters of faith (*ST* I,
> 94, 3c).

We can have natural knowledge that the only
thing that will pacify us is some sort of activ-

ity in accordance with virtue, completely realized in complete life (cf. *ST* I-II, 3, 2c). But we can learn about that sort of activity only by faith, and can share in it only by grace.

> [T]he final happiness *(beatitudo)* prepared for the saints surpasses both the intellect and the will of man. *Eye hath not seen, nor ear heard, neither hath it entered into the heart of man, what things God hath prepared for them that love him* (*ST* I-II, 5, 5c).

In this way, Aristotle's theory of the end of human life, while preserved, is transformed.[22]

5. Divine Comedy

St. Thomas's transformation of Aristotle's theory of happiness also transforms the problem whether human life is ultimately tragic. Not, however, by finding anything ethically impossible in its being tragic.

The cardinal point in St. Thomas's theory is that the ultimate end of human life is not the state of blessedness reached when the vision of God is attained, but is pre-existent, God himself. There is no logical repugnance in the supposition that God should so have ordered things that human beings would perish at death like other animals. If so, their desire to know God directly would never be satisfied; and they would never gain complete happiness. Yet God would exist for all that. And although human beings could not attain their ultimate end through their own operation, in knowing and loving God, they could, like the rest of creation, participate in the divine perfection according to their nature, which although intellectual, is finite and corporeal. They could understand enough of the moral life and of the physical world – including that it is created by an infinite first cause – to deserve to be called the paragon of animals. Nothing created, not even the knowing and loving of God by created beings, increases the amount of goodness that exists. If God alone existed things would be as good as they now are. God has no need to create anything (cf. *SCG* I, 81, 2-4; *ST* I, 104, 3c). A created world in which human beings at best gain the human happiness Aristotle describes would not be repugnant to practical reason.

St. Thomas, if I have reconstructed his position correctly, held that, from the point of view of human beings, things are unimaginably better than philosophy gives them any reason to hope. To those who agree with the great scientist and (humanly speaking) good man, William Kingdon Clifford, that it is a moral duty to dismiss any opinion that cannot be demonstrated, St. Thomas did wrong in accepting the Christian revelation without scientific or philosophical demonstration. I do not think he did. Nor do I think that, in order to justify disagreeing with Clifford, we must resort, like William James, to arguing that, when a proposition cannot be demonstrated to be either true or false, we are entitled to believe whatever makes for beneficial results in practice.[23] On this topic, however, I cannot here say much. Assuming that a divine creator is not a philosophical impossibility, if such a creator should reveal himself to intellectual creatures (as in the alleged revelation of the Torah to Moses), I do not see how authenticity of that revelation could be *philosophically* demonstrated. As long as we cannot see God directly, he can only reveal himself by signs; and, from the point of view of philosophy, signs are intractably ambiguous. A theory here is certainly needed. And no doubt philosophy has something to contribute to developing one; but such a theory could not strictly be a part of philosophy.

If my argument is sound, St. Thomas held that Aristotle was mistaken when he main-

tained that the ultimate end of human life is
what *he* called *eudaimonia.* Apart from revelation, the ultimate end is God, and the image
of God in every human being. Naturally, like
all living things, human beings also seek, by
such means as they think permissible, the
telos that is theirs by nature — *eudaimonia.*
But even though, by grace, they so act in this
life as to attain their ultimate end in the next,
they may nevertheless fail to attain anything
Aristotle would have described as *eudaimonia.* Of course, what Aristotle accounted
a failure, St. Thomas did not. He saved Aristotle's thesis that the ultimate end of human
life is *eudaimonia* by two drastic amend-
ments. First, he reinterpreted *eudaimonia* as
what he called *beatitudo*: the total satisfac-
tion of the desires of an intellectual creature
by a vision of God's essence unmediated by
any intermediary *species intelligibilis* or concept. Secondly, he denied that human beings
could either attain *beatitudo,* or even learn
what it really is, except by grace. *Beatitudo,*
so understood, is not only a far greater thing
than Aristotle ever thought *eudaimonia* to be,
but it is in principle attainable by all human
beings, no matter what their birth or fortune

in life. Saved in this way, of course, the thesis ceases to be a philosophical one.

A final thought. In view of his theory of its ultimate end, Aristotle could not but conclude that human life is a failure for most of us, and a tragedy for many of the best of us. In doing so, he was sagacious as well as candid. By contrast, the efforts of two of the best of his successors, Kant and Sidgwick, to reach a conclusion more cheerful than his, were at best excusable. St. Thomas's way of making Aristotle's teaching cheerful, while it would have been as foolish to the Greeks as St. Paul's theology was, has the merit of being inexcusable.

Notes

The texts of the two works of St. Thomas I used throughout are:

> (i) *Summa contra Gentiles*. Editio Leonina manualis. Turin and Rome: Casa Editrice Marietta, 1946. Abbreviated as '*SCG*'.

> (ii) *Summa Theologiae*. 60 vols. London and New York: Blackfriars, in conjunction with Eyre and Spottiswoode and McGraw Hill, 1963-76. (General Index issued in 1981 as vol. 61.) Abbreviated as '*ST*'.

Responsibility for translations is mine. However, in *Summa contra Gentiles,* of which I quote only from Parts I and III, I follow fairly closely the renderings of Anton C. Pegis and Vernon J. Bourke in the edition in five volumes republished by the University of Notre Dame Press in 1975. Most of my renderings of *Summa Theologiae* take those of the Blackfriars edition as their point of departure, but are usually more literal.

1. John Duns Scotus, *De primo Principio*. Revised text and translation by Evan Roche OFM. St. Bonaventure, N.Y.: the Franciscan Institute (1949), ch. 2, concl. 5 (pp. 116-19). Although I should have been helpless without Fr. Roche's version, I have made bold to depart from it, hoping that my revised version would be more intelligible when read aloud.

Scotus's text, from which I have translated excerpts, is as follows:

Probatur: quia finis non est causa nisi inquantum ab ipso tamquam a priore essentialiter dependet esse finiti. Patet, quia quaelibet causa est sic prior inquantum causa. Non autem dependet finitum quantum ad esse a fine ut sic priore, nisi inquantum finis ut amatus movet efficiens ad dandum illi esse, ita quod efficiens non daret esse in suo genere nisi fine causante in sua causalitate. Nihil ergo causat finis, nisi quod efficitur ab efficiente qua amante finem.

Hic corollarium sequitur non tacendum, quod falsa imaginatio est de fine, quod illud est causa finalis entis, quod est operatio ultima vel objectum, quod per illam operationem attingitur. Si intelligatur quod tale inquantum tale est causa finalis, falsum est, quia illud consequitur esse; nec esse finiti dependet essentialiter ab illo inquantum tale, sed praecise illud, propter quod amatum ab efficiente, efficiens facit aliquid esse, quia ordinatum ad amatum, illud inquantum est causa finalis facti.

2. *Summa Theologiae* I-II, 1, 8c.

3. *Summa Theologiae* I-II, 100, 6c.

4. Sir David Ross, *Kant's Ethical Theory.* Oxford: Clarendon Press (1959), p. 51.

5. Cf. David Hume, *Enquiries into the Human Understanding and into the Principles of Morals.* Ed. L.A. Selby-Bigge. 2nd edn. Oxford: Clarendon Press (1902), pp. 221-22, 272-79.

6. In "Is Thomas Aquinas a Natural Law Ethicist?" *Monist* 18 (1974): 52-66, Vernon J. Bourke surveys the corpus of St. Thomas's ethical writings, and usefully comments on differences between them. He confesses that, as a result, "the theory of right reason seems to me to take precendence [in St. Thomas's work] over the theory of natural law" (p. 66). This concedes too much to anti-rationalist con-

ceptions of law. To St. Thomas, I suspect, Professor Bourke's distinction would be without a difference.

7. Henry Sidgwick, *The Methods of Ethics*. 7th edn. London: Macmillan, (1907), p. 411.

8. Ibid., p. 121.

9. Jerome B. Schneewind, *Sidgwick's Ethics and Victorian Moral Theory*. Oxford: Clarendon Press (1977), ch. 13, is the best treatment of these topics. Cf. my review essay, 'A New Sidgwick?' in *Ethics* 90 (1980): 282-95, esp. 288-89 and 294-95.

10. Sidgwick, *Methods of Ethics,* p. 508.

11. Ibid.

12. Ibid.

13. Ibid., p. 509.

14. Immanuel Kant, *Kritik der praktischen Vernunft*. Riga: Hartnoch (1788), pp. 198-99. (Akad. edn. Vol. V, p. 110.) Tr. L.W. Beck.

15. Ibid. p. 202. (Akad. edn., p. 113.) Tr. Beck.

16. Ibid. p. 205. (Akad. edn., p. 114.) Tr. Beck.

17. Ithaca, N.Y.: Cornell University Press (1970).

18. Wood, *Kant's Moral Religion,* p. 226.

19. Aristotle, *Nicomachean Ethics* I, 1101a 18-22; quoted by St. Thomas, *ST* I-II, 3, 2 ad 4.

20. Bertrand Russell, *The Analysis of Mind*. London: Allen and Unwin, 1921. Cf. C.D. Broad, *Examination of McTaggart's Philosophy,* Vol. I. Cambridge: Cambridge University Press (1933), p. li.

21. Russell, *Analysis of Mind,* pp. 65-68.

22. In pointing out the limits of Aristotle's conception of *eudaimonia* as the end of human life, I do not think that I have asserted anything that Aristotelians who are also Thomists would deny. But they

do not assert it – or not as stridently as I do. Cf. Henry B. Veatch, *Rational Man* (Bloomington: Indiana University Press, 1962), pp. 177-79; and *Aristotle* (Bloomington: Indiana University Press, 1974), pp. 103-11, 124-27.

23. William James, in his essay "The Will to Believe," originally published in the *New World,* June 1896, quoted Clifford at length in developing his alternative view. The version I have used is that in William James, *Essays in Pragmatism,* ed. Alburey Castell. New York: Hafner (1948).

Published by the Marquette University Press
Milwaukee, Wisconsin 53233
United States of America

#1 St. Thomas and the Life of Learning (1937)
by John F. McCormick, S.J. (1874-1943)
professor of philosophy, Loyola University.
ISBN 0-87462-101-1

#2 St. Thomas and the Gentiles (1938) by Mortimer J. Adler, Ph.D., Director of the Institute of Philosophical Research, San Francisco, Calif.   ISBN 0-87462-102-X

#3 St. Thomas and the Greeks (1939) by Anton C. Pegis, Ph.D., professor of philosophy, Pontifical Institute of Mediaeval Studies, Toronto.   ISBN 0-87462-103-8

#4 The Nature and Functions of Authority (1940) by Yves Simon, Ph.D., (1903-1961) professor of philosophy of social thought, University of Chicago.   ISBN 0-87462-104-6

#5 St. Thomas and Analogy (1941) by Gerald B. Phelan, Ph.D., (1892-1965) professor of philosophy, St. Michael's College, Toronto.
ISBN 0-87462-105-4

#6 St. Thomas and the Problem of Evil (1942) by Jacques Maritain, Ph.D., professor *emeritus* of philosophy, Princeton University.
ISBN 0-87462-106-2

#7 Humanism and Theology (1943) by Werner Jaeger, Ph.D., Litt.D., (1888-1961) University professor, Harvard University.
ISBN 0-87462-107-0

#8　The Nature and Origins of Scientism (1944) by John Wellmuth, Chairman of the Department of Philosophy, Loyola University.
ISBN 0-87462-108-9

#9　Cicero in the Courtroom of St. Thomas Aquinas (1945) by E. K. Rand, Ph.D., Litt D., LL.D. (1871-1945) Pope professor of Latin, *emeritus,* Harvard University.　ISBN 0-87462-109-7

#10　St. Thomas and Epistemology (1946) by Louis-Marie Regis, O.P., Th.L., Ph.D., director of the Albert the Great Institute of Mediaeval Studies, University of Montreal.
ISBN 0-87462-110-0

#11　St. Thomas and the Greek Moralists (1947, Spring) by Vernon J. Bourke, Ph.D., professor of philosophy, St. Louis University, St. Louis, Missouri.　ISBN 0-87462-111-9

#12　History of Philosophy and Philosophical Education (1947, Fall) by Etienne Gilson of the *Académie français,* director of studies and professor of the history of Mediaeval philosophy, Pontifical Institute of Mediaeval Studies, Toronto.　ISBN 0-87462-112-7

#13　The Natural Desire for God (1948) by William R. O'Connor, S.T.L., Ph.D., former professor of dogmatic theology, St. Joseph's Seminary, Dunwoodie, N.Y.　ISBN 0-87462-113-5

#14　St. Thomas and the World State (1949) by Robert M. Hutchins, former Chancellor of the University of Chicago, president, of the Fund for the Republic.　ISBN 0-87462-114-3

#15　Method in Metaphysics (1950) by Robert J. Henle, S.J., Ph.D., academic vice-president, St. Louis University, St. Louis, Missouri.
ISBN 0-87462-115-1

#24 Metaphysics and Ideology (1959) by Wm. Oliver Martin, Ph.D., professor of philosophy, University of Rhode Island.
ISBN 0-87462-124-0

#25 Language, Truth and Poetry (1960) by Victor M. Hamm, Ph.D., professor of English, Marquette University. ISBN 0-87462-125-9

#26 Metaphysics and Historicity (1961) by Emil L. Fackenheim, Ph.D., professor of philosophy, University of Toronto.
ISBN 0-87462-126-7

#27 The Lure of Wisdom (1962) by James D. Collins, Ph.D., professor of philosophy, St. Louis University. ISBN 0-87462-127-5

#28 Religion and Art (1963) by Paul Weiss, Ph.D. Sterling professor of philosophy, Yale University. ISBN 0-87462-128-3

#29 St. Thomas and Philosophy (1964) by Anton C. Pegis, Ph.D., professor of philosophy, Pontifical Institute of Mediaeval Studies, Toronto. ISBN 0-87462-129-1

#30 The University in Process (1965) by John O. Riedl, Ph.D., dean of faculty, Queensboro Community College. ISBN 0-87462-130-5

#31 The Pragmatic Meaning of God (1966) by Robert O. Johann, associate professor of philosophy, Fordham University.
ISBN 0-87462-131-3

#32 Religion and Empiricism (1967) by John E. Smith, Ph.D., professor of philosophy, Yale University. ISBN 0-87462-132-1

#33 The Subject (1968) by Bernard Lonergan, S.J., S.T.D., professor of dogmatic theory, Regis College, Ontario and Gregorian University, Rome.   ISBN 0-87462-133-X

#34 Beyond Trinity (1969) by Bernard J. Cooke, S.J., S.T.D., Marquette University.
                                   ISBN 0-87462-134-8

#35 Ideas and Concepts (1970) by Julius R. Weinberg, Ph.D., (1908-1971) Vilas Professor of Philosophy, University of Wisconsin.
                                   ISBN 0-87462-135-6

#36 Reason and Faith Revisited (1971) by Francis H. Parker, Ph.D., head of the philosophy department, Purdue University, Lafayette, Indiana.   ISBN 0-87462-136-4

#37 Psyche and Cerebrum (1972) by John N. Findlay, M.A. Oxon, Ph.D., Clark Professor of Moral Philosophy and Metaphysics, Yale University.   ISBN 0-87462-137-2

#38 The Problem of the Criterion (1973) by Roderick M. Chisholm, Ph.D., Andrew W. Mellon, Professor in the Humanities, Brown University.   ISBN 0-87462-138-0

#39 Man as Infinite Spirit (1974) by James H. Robb, Ph.D., professor of philosophy, Marquette University.   ISBN 0-87462-139-9

#40 Aquinas to Whitehead: Seven Centuries of Metaphysics of Religion (1976) by Charles E. Hartshorne, Ph.D., professor of philosophy, the University of Texas at Austin.
                                   ISBN 0-87462-141-0

#41 The Problem of Evil (1977) by Errol E. Harris, D.Litt., Distinguished Visiting Professor of Philosophy, Marquette University.
                                   ISBN 0-87462-142-9

#42 The Catholic University and the Faith (1978) by Francis C. Wade, S.J., professor of philosophy, Marquette University.

ISBN 0-87462-143-7

#43 St. Thomas and Historicity (1979) by Armand Maurer, C.S.B., professor of philosophy, University of Toronto and the Pontifical Institute of Mediaeval Studies, Toronto.

ISBN 0-87462-144-5

#44 Does God Have a Nature? (1980) by Alvin Plantinga, Ph.D., professor of philosophy, Calvin College, Grand Rapids, Michigan.

ISBN 0-87462-145-3

#45 Rhyme and Reason: St. Thomas and Modes of Discourse (1981) by Ralph McInerny, Ph.D., professor of Medieval Studies, University of Notre Dame.   ISBN 0-87462-148-8

#46 The Gift: Creation (1982) by Kenneth L. Schmitz, Ph.D., professor of philosophy at Trinity College, University of Toronto.

ISBN 0-87462-149-6

#47 How Philosophy Begins (1983) by Beatrice H. Zedler, Ph.D., professor of philosophy, Marquette University.

ISBN 0-87462-151-8

#48 The Reality of the Historical Past (1984) by Paul Ricoeur, professor of philosophy, University of Paris.

ISBN 0-87462-152-6

#49 Human Ends and Human Actions (1985) by Alan Donagan, professor of philosophy at the California Institute of Technology.

ISBN 0-87462-153-4

Uniform format, cover and binding.

Copies of this Aquinas Lecture and the others in the series are obtainable from:

Marquette University Press
Marquette University
Milwaukee, Wisconsin 53233, U.S.A.